MUDDY WINGS

Copyright Shandle Chapman

Published by Shandle Chapman

Printed in the United States of America

Manufactured in the United States of America

Library of Congress Cataloging-in-Publication Data is Available

ISBN: 978-0-578-46863-1

Imprint: Independently published

A renewed mindset lifts the weight off your wings.

MUDDY WINGS

A POETIC COLLECTION OF THOUGHTS

SHANDLE CHAPMAN

Contents

- Taken Away
- Cover
- That One Time
- Lime Light
- After Her
- Mannequins
- Demented Love
- Triggers
- Zaire
- Still
- Ten on Two
- His Frustration
- What's Best
- High Discoveries
- My Candle
- Toe to Toe
- Different Gears
- Playing It Safe
- Conscientious
- Wind then the Rain
- Hydroplane

Part II: Tune Up

God thank you for direction, clarity, and unyielding faithfulness. Thank you for giving me the strength I needed to come forward with my story. Thank you for this opportunity.

You are my hiding place; you will protect me from trouble and surround me with songs of deliverance.
Psalms 32:7

Dedication

My writing influences. My interest in poetry began when I was a teenager. I was inspired to write for many reasons. I wrote my first poem after the death of a family friend and I have been a writer ever since.

I would like to thank my children Jeremiah and Maurice for their unwavering love and understanding throughout this entire process. You are the reasons why I am determined to speak out about my truth. You aided this journey and kept my desires oxygenated. It is my obligation to uplift you and make you aware of the realities of this world. My prayer is that you live an abundant life and never undergo suffering in silence or wait to release any hurt that seems inescapable. I pray that you recognize and embrace challenges that contribute to your wellbeing and disregard those that attempt to hamper a fulfilling life. I pray that you experience growth through lessons, capture the freedom of knowledge and continue to remain strong in your faith.

To my Mother and Father, thank you for being the parents that I need. Most patient, God fearing, understanding, and loving without conditions. You have allowed me to discover me, while never leaving my side. Your love and support planted seeds of courage and I cannot thank you enough. I am forever indebted.

I want to thank the readers of this book for taking interest in my craft. Please share this book of poetry with anyone you feel it may help or inspire. May peace and joy be with you.

Foreword

What this book means. Muddy Wings is an amazing creation of poetry connected to personal struggles, thoughts, and decisions. It depicts a journey of events and observations made during challenging stages of my life. The mud symbolizes circumstances and hindrances faced, while the wings represent self-discovery and healing, which was the byproduct of owning a renewed mindset. Muddy Wings is designed to convey how my mental state affected my personal development and the message is delivered through the art of poetry.

In this book of poetry, I boldly place contributing factors on display, some of which were avoidable and others not so much. Ultimately realizing that the experiences were on replay because they were permitted to be.

Do tell. After walking a long road of bad decisions, I rested and made peace with myself. I was tired of the circles and chasing desires located within arm's reach, so I decided to reflect. In doing so, I had to acknowledge my faults, understand my purpose and realize that it was not the end. It was time for me to reset and plunge into what was destine for me. I had to decide between giving up and pushing through despite the agony. The task was difficult, one of the most difficult things I had ever done for myself, but it was overdue. It meant that I had to believe, stay the course, and remove anything that kept me motionless, starting with my thoughts. It meant that I had to stop dreaming of the dream and start living it. My mindset needed to change, and my actions had to follow.

When I began the process of self-reflection, I recognized signs of depression. Although not clinically diagnosed, dealing with depression made life more challenging and less enjoyable. Through research I became aware of the signs and symptoms of depression which most often stem from other mental health disorders. In my case, anxiety was the contributing factor of my emotional distress. I often faced self-inflicted blockage which caused me to have fluctuating energy. During this period persistence was a missing component, I second guessed my abilities, and nothing kept me motivated long enough to complete a task. Fear was my antagonist and I promoted my own downfalls. As a result, my desires appeared out of reach and I didn't make the best decisions. I became impatient with myself, shame and self-pity engulfed me, and anxiety kept me stagnant. Despite the relentless image I maintained, I struggled through sadness and a negative self-thought process. Doubting my abilities was a continuous practice due to my own distorted beliefs. The combination of failed attempts and lack of movement took me deeper into a sunken place. I felt weak in so many areas of my life, but my custom-made disguise supplied my strength. In my weakest moments, my smile was perfect for hiding my internal frown. I mastered the ability to appear happier than I was, and I absorbed troubles that I did not own. My struggles remained consistent because my efforts remained inconsistent until I changed my mindset.

Part I: Box of Chocolates

M.U.D
Many Unfortunate Decisions

Don't be so hard on yourself,
Look forward to the new day,
Shake it off and carry on,
A blessing is coming your way.

You're stuck in the mud, but not for long,
You're a diamond in the rough,
Say a prayer and hold on.

The power of decisions and the energy manifested
through those decisions bring awareness to your strengths
and potential. Decisions shape your life and most often
result in experiences embedded with lessons that help you
understand who you are.

Hone in on positive thoughts and you'll experience things
that help you get through your rough days.

To My Grave

How did this become an assignment?
Maybe, I should say when,
I don't ask many questions these days,
I just walk around and pretend,
That everything is ok, even though it's not,
Someday these thoughts will catch up with me,
Forgiving is easy, but I haven't forgot.

The flap that will not lay,
Keeps blowing in the wind,
It's an envelope I want to seal, a letter I want to send,
The wound that never heals because the scab was pulled
again,
Dialogue I want to have, to bring this to an end.

Sunken in desolation, waiting on the seasons ahead for
propitious inspiration,
On the account of experiences, that chanted,
condemnation;
Exposed through actions nobody could see,
Brewed into a promiscuous transmission of energy.

Ridicule blocked my sunshine,
Obstruction tingled my toes,
Inside is where the sentiment remained captive,
Conforming to what was retroactive;
Tainting the desire for companionship and injuring trust,
Through furnished mental destruction with esteem coated
in dust;
Significantly changing the intended path with ripples of
energy that didn't last.

I stood in the doorway as if I owed a debt,
Framed by a stony face, though inside I wept;
Wishing to redirect the focus, and incessantly wondering why.
What made me the choice?
I thought you were a good guy.
Finding no logical reason,
For why it ever started,
Trying to find my out, since my energy already departed.
Overwhelmed with confusion,
Optimistic of the phase,
Reluctant to speak out,
Then it suddenly went away.

I was greeted with relief when it ended.
I'll figure out the reason, there's no need to explain,
I'll bury it six feet deep and never mention your name;
Your character will be saved,
I will take it to my grave.

Captain Crunch

When I get high, I eat Captain Crunch,
I'm on my fifth bowl without milk, I ran out;
I'm wise when I'm high, I just hope it last,
This is some good stuff because my thoughts are moving
fast.

The journey I embark, only I can understand,
My creativity gleams, and my knowledge, it expands.
My talents seem never ending, they clearly enhance.
I'm not making this up, just ask my man;
I excel when I'm high, and it's not a joke,
I'm driven and ambitious as hell when I smoke.

Leave my high alone, just let me vibe,
You don't know the things that I'm holding inside;
My high writes passionately,
The pencil spirals with adequacy,
The cadence of my cardiac rhythm speeds,
Writing is a drug that my psyche needs.

The windows to my soul become fixated on operational
flow,
Sailing in a forward direction, but never too fast or slow,
Drawn into the hypnotic structure that broadens my
dreams,
Organizing a list of those loyal to my team.
Between the lines and within the margins,
The bandage is removed and doubt discarded,
I take a moment to remember how it all started.

My muse, my passion,

Lights, cameras, action.
I was only 14 when I first got high,
In remembrance of a crush, who is now in the sky.

I boarded this ship when I had no clue,
Then I wondered, lacking confidence, as I always do.
Second guessing my abilities, instead of flying to the moon,
What if, but if, I'm not ready, it's too soon.
Now, my high is gone, the wave has disappeared,
I have failed again at being the Captain of my ship.

If History

They say history repeats itself, but what does that mean.
Maybe, it means that we, could be living in our dream,
Achieving mostly anything, and uncovering the truth,
Relentlessly creating a path for our youth,
Assuming our purpose would be clear, with teachings for
every ear to hear;
From generation to generation,
Finally understanding what it means to be one nation;
Jumping over hurdles to reach the unseen,
Working diligently to build a phenomenal team;
Focusing on the prize without an excuse,
Absorbing knowledge that we can never lose;
Laying pavements and upgrading our skills,
Seeking fulfilment through a power stronger than four
wheels.

If history repeats itself, should we rush the task,
Should we ask questions that have already been asked,
Should we expect peace and equality to last?
Will we become immune to the flow of rejection?
Constantly stigmatized by our rich complexion.
Will the disassociation ever end?
Will conviction continue because of the melanin in our
skin?
Should we ever expect equal rights after emancipation,
Will we ever stand tall enough to create innovation?
Maybe nothing will change, only coated and covered to
avoid the appearance of one in the same.
Maybe, we'll be forced to put up a fight,
Our achievements will be downplayed, but they'll
broadcast our plight.

Can You

The last 24 hours have been hard for me. I've had to wrap my mind around the fact that you've been cheating on me for several months. While all of the evidence presented bothers me, what bothers me most is that you treated me as though I've betrayed you,

No, I don't want an explanation and I don't need an apology. I just want to be left alone.

Can you do that for me?

Can you tell that I trying to keep it together?
Although I wasn't prepared for this stormy weather.

Can you allow me to move pass this pain? To keep me from thinking all men are the same.

Can you let go so I can find my way out? I loved you dearly without any doubts.

Can you take all the moments we shared and try to imagine me not being there?

Can you ignore your emotion and all of your thoughts? Let me be the one you've completely forgot.

Can you?

Critical Elevation

Smoking with the train that just went by,
Making use of my third eye;
Judging my downfalls and delaying my truth.
Behind, behind, behind, behind,
The word that leases room in my mind.
It alters my plans and redirects my path.
The result of tippy-toeing into my desires,
I'm filled with energy, but partially inspired.
Planted for reasons of my own,
Regretting the time that I've blown;
Running away from everything that I don't understand,
Constantly falling, into the arms of a man,
Expecting to be healed from wounds I allowed myself to
withstand.

Wondering how to turn things around,
Tired of the fake laughs and concealed frowns,
It's time to clap and stop letting myself down.
Since I cannot count on anyone else,
I must push harder to encourage myself;
To generate plays and take open shots,
I have tried several times, but I messed up a lot.

The possibilities are endless for celebrating a new day,
Staying the course right after I pray;
Discipling myself and displaying my glow,
Exercising my strengths and respecting the flow,
Sharpening aptitudes needed to surpass,

With the intent to spread knowledge from under the
grass;
Picking myself up and adjusting my crown,
This is it, I can no longer let myself down.

Bottle

A bottle a day makes the pain go away,
On top of that, I still pray.
Don't judge me,
What's in your cup?
Mine has dreams of a woman who won't give up;
A bottle a day is why my skin is so dry,
On top of that I like to get high,
Yeah, I look good, but I'm living a lie;
This bottle helps me deal with my truth,
I don't care if subtracts days from my youth;
It makes promises that I'll never forget,
Sometimes I even post them on the internet.
My senses increase when I'm sipping slow,
While I'm writing and tipping my glass of merlot;
I can drink a whole bottle by myself,
As I turn it up and imagine my wealth.
Bye, bye bottle, I'm almost threw,
Without you, I wouldn't know what I would do;
The sun is rising, and I didn't get any sleep,
I'll see you tomorrow, in my glass is where we'll meet.

Havoc

Self-destruction, you're gonna cause self-destruction.

She pressed repeat, but not to comprehend,
A behavior unlearned, self-sabotage again.
Mend what I didn't break and take the blame,
Or continue as I have, insisting that, "It's not my fault"
with no shame.
Research your target, my wit is my gun,
While your blood pressure rises, I do this for fun.
Interrupt my peace and havoc will invade your space,
They always underestimate this cute face.

My Last Days

I gave what was due, I was good to you
Loyalty and affection despite your neglection.
My heart was all in,
Now, where should I begin.
At the beginning when our love was explosive;
In the middle when you chose to cheat, and I stayed;
Maybe towards the end, when you finally decided to be
supportive of the path,
I put in work, so you do the math;
Maybe I became comfortable far too soon,
I gave you my truth under the moon,
The relentless energy that flowed in my veins,
Until they collapsed from the constant pain,
Hands of abhorrence established an uninvited phase,
Left me with no choice, except to give you my last days.

Facade

Smiling through sadness,
Hiding in the cold,
Don't believe the facade, watch the windows to my soul.
I'm happy when I dream, but it all ends there,
Attempting to decipher the moment as I stare.
Taken out of space and feeling displaced.
Micromanaging this false reflection,
My thoughts move quickly toward regression.
Nonetheless, I smile unsuspectingly wide,
Impressed by my ability to maneuver as I hide.
Throughout the setbacks and endless strife,
I learned to adapt and balance the problems in my life.
The defense mechanisms that made me feel ok,
Smiling and writing seemed to make it go away.
The lack of concentration, and emotions buried deep,
The hill of self-reflection was tall and steep.
Masked by a veil which made it appear to be fine,
Structured for my parents, who worried most of the time.
It was always enough, to make life worth living,
When the next day came, I challenged the mood I was
given.

What Did I Do

When frustrations hit,
I often yelled and cursed.
Sometimes so intensely, a blood vessel was bound to
burst.
The energy I gave off wasn't anything new,
At that moment, you were the blame for everything I was
going through.
Afterwards, I felt bad, the guilt coated my insides,
Fixed on being upset, but I wanted to apologize.
All the things I said, I felt you needed to improve,
Issues I only mentioned when I felt discomfort in my
shoes.
You looked at me in curiosity and asked, what did I do.
I never admitted that you did nothing wrong,
Although you were the first to see the reaction of the hurt,
I kept stringing along.

I apologize,

Jeremiah and Maurice

Reciprocity

I don't hate that I love you, but sometimes I fight the
feeling,
That is when I stop to consider the deck of cards you've
been dealing.
It's hard to receive what you've never understood,
Consistency and devotion when the seasons aren't good.
I made sure you knew no tricks were up my sleeves,
Although I was never subscribed as the one you'll always
need.
I willingly gave my love to remove any doubt,
What I wanted in return were the things that I put out,
Fire and desire is what it was all about.
If you couldn't handle it, you should've let me know,
Since communication is key to helping us learn and grow.
I never wanted to be the reason you wore an internal
frown,
I never wanted you to identify me as the one who forced
you to stay around.
The appreciation shown depends on who's involved,
I seemed to create all the problems you never cared solve.
I ran over the signs, just to set the tone,
Even though your energy made me realize I was in this
alone.
There was fear that contributed to our initial start,
Which should've been removed because you knew you
had my heart.

However, it didn't resonate so your actions remained flat,
Still, I continued trying and cut you some slack.

My only expectation was for you to contribute to our
cause,
It all seemed realistic until I decided to pause.

In the Bed

Your hopes and dreams are not in this bed,
Get up and go, you have a bright future ahead.
The fetal position you lay in has you stuck,
Thinking about your sins and wanting to give up.
Your goals can't be reached if you don't touch the floor,
Have you even wondered why your keeping score;
Don't compare your life, your mission is different,
The things you endure, others aren't built for it.
He knows how much to put on your plate,
Believe me when I say, he makes no mistakes.
Make use of your time and construct a plan,
Instead of laying in the bed under the ceiling fan.

She Didn't Know

The visits were not frequent, and I don't remember much,
I recall her being tall, long hair, and soft to touch.
She said it was ok and directed my innocent hand,
My hesitation was her fuel, it activated her plan.
She came into the room, shortly after I arrived,
Insisting that I stayed to watch from the other side;
She undressed in front of me, never appearing to be ashamed,
She was supposed to be family, at least that's what they claimed.
Each time I went to that house, I drifted into space,
I wish my parents would've known it wasn't a safe place.
A reaction was expected, so one was what she got,
I was far too young to learn the location of a g spot.
I couldn't understand why she introduced me to this world,
I wasn't ready for the experience, I was just a little girl.
Trouble is what I predicted, so I kept my mouth closed,
Each time they planned for my stay, I didn't know how to oppose;
The energy she transferred was all that she had,
Now, I realize she was broken, and her influences were bad.
She didn't know the effect it would have on me prolonged,
Or the subconscious stigma she was passing along.
There was no telling what she had been through, but she gave vivid examples of all that she knew.

Unconditional Hurt

Where is my makeup,
I can't find my makeup,
Who has my makeup,
I need to cover this bruise,
I need to cover this black eye,
I need my makeup,
Where is my makeup,
I need to pretend everything is ok,
I want people think my home is happy,
I need my makeup,
Where is my makeup,
I need to go out in public,
I want to go to the store,
People will talk about me,
Where's my makeup,
I need my makeup,
I don't want my family to question me,
I don't want my friends to know,
They'll tell me he's no good for me,
Where is my makeup,
I need my makeup,
I can't tell anyone what really happened,
They won't understand,
They'll tell me to leave him,
They'll lock up my man,
Where's my makeup,
I need my makeup,
He's just protecting me,
It's for my own good,

Where is my makeup,

Shandle Chapman   **Muddy Wings**

I can't find my makeup,
I don't need your help,
I have a place to go to,
Where is my makeup,
I can't find my makeup,
He came home with roses,
He bought my favorite chocolates,
We made love to slow jams,
Where is my makeup,
I can't find my makeup,
He said he didn't mean it,
I believe him,
Yes, I'm fine
It doesn't hurt that bad, the pain will go away over time,
I need my makeup,
Where is my makeup,
I need start my day,
I must walk with my head up and paste a smile on my face.
Where is my makeup.

Taken Away

Wait, don't take them,
Then again, go ahead,
I shouldn't, but it's best,
At least that's what he said;
I can't stand up because he knocked me down,
My self-esteem splattered across the ground.
I'm the blame, it's my fault, I'm the one who let you go;
Afterall, it was in my womb, that you tried to grow,
Planted into whom you'd never know.
Hoping a seed would make him stay,
His concern was that you'd be in the way;
Not once did I take a moment to pray, but I took the city
bus on that day.
Of course, he wasn't there, but his encouragement was
strong,
A devoted fan of his desired plan, cheering me along.
Protestors were marching on the sidewalks straight ahead,
Holding up large signs, chanting and reciting what God
said.
My thoughts were everywhere, I didn't think it through,
My head was spinning, I didn't know what to do,
Emotional instability began to brew.
I wanted to run in the opposite direction,
Then I found a tunnel beyond their protection,
Forcing myself to adopt a feeling of total disconnection.

I run up the stairs and shut the door behind,
Telling myself it'll be over soon, and I'll be fine.
My senses returned after the act,
Although it was too late to turn the clock back.
It took no time for the sin to haunt me deep,

Shandle Chapman   **Muddy Wings**

While getting dressed, I began to weep;
Of course, I knew better, of course I did,

I played house, but I never played God as a kid;

The evidence was discarded and taken away,
The room felt dark with no streaks of ray;
Everything happened in the blink of an eye,
Alone and ashamed to look up to the sky;
The signs were gone, but I wanted to hide,
Concerned with who may have seen me go inside;
The lesson that followed, opened my eyes wide,
I am not He who has the power to decide.

When I broke down, I will never forget,
The guilt and hurt that made me repent.

Cover

I recently met a man who seemed different from the rest,
He was nicely dressed, and his speech was not a mess;
His cufflinks shined bright,
His eyes said, goodnight;
Mr. Chestnut fine,
Ready to have a good time;
We talked on the phone and I heard myself moan,
What am I to do?
He appears interesting and new,
Then I paused for a moment, before continuing through,
Taking a closer look from a microscopic view.
Magnifying the hurt endured in several ways,
Often blowing it off through the substance he blazed.
Guarded and reluctant to give his best;
Going into relationships, with bullet proof vest;
Breaking love down and repeating the past,
With hidden intentions that surface fast,
Bitterness and pain filled with vapors from the rain,
The hurt he tried to cover ran deep in his veins,
There must be a cure for all this pain,
A slight difference, but still one in the same.
Unable to trust from betrayal submerged deep,
Dealt with in isolation until resting in peace.

This experience taught me that men cover up hurt and
pain too. Recognize that a man needs to heal before he
passes that hurt onto you. Forcing a relationship upon a
man will not allow him to display his best self because he
is not his best self. I had to realize this and in doing so I
had to let go.

That One Time

I was finger printed and booked after telling them to go to hell,
The charge was disorderly conduct, but I don't remember the bail,
They said, one phone call was all that I had,
At that moment my memory became extremely bad;
On the opposite end, the voice told me not to cry,
Tears will show weakness so keep those eyes dry;
I said, ok, and hung up with a frown,
Patiently waiting, for something to go down;
I saw a few that I knew from the block,
I guess that meant, my block was hot;
Those cheap panties are all I remember,
They welcomed my vagina as the newest member;
The county jail scared me straight,
They sent a sandwich to the pod, since it was late;
Although I was there for less than twenty-four hours,
I hurried home and took a long shower;
You couldn't tell me I wasn't a thug when I left,
As I walked to the bus stop, staying to myself,
Don't mess with me, I just got out of jail,
You see my clear bag, I'm crazy as hell;
This mouth of mine got me in this situation,
I never thought of the time I'd be facing,
That one time I went to jail.

Limelight

Her transition was smooth into the limelight,
She focused on her grind and didn't stay all night;
Selecting custom-made outfits to fit her physique,
When she hit center stage, six inches were on her feet.
Influenced by the units in total control,
A venue marked for survival, a hustle for the bold.
Skin coated with makeup, primed with dignity,
Entering an environment requiring immense agility.
The temporary plan that drifted into years,
Gaining fast profit through the fantasy she gives.
Empathizing with lies and gifting with gab,
Observing the monetary flow of those who have a tab.
Visions of lust and persuasion was the setup,
Once hooked in, typically they wouldn't let up.
Creating an interaction kept them coming back,
To single her out and spend at least a stack.
The thickness of the ambiance set in smoke,
The orders of henny chased with coke.
Currency cascading and causing puddles,
Dancers disagreeing and inducing trouble.
The limelight shines bright with false affection,
But if you grind, you won't face rejection.

After Her

He found ticket stubs in her purse, although he didn't go,
Which confirmed his gut feeling and he felt compelled to
let me know.
The number was unfamiliar and still I picked up,
My ears bleed heavily, the information was abrupt.
My heart was deceived and this he could tell,
If the issue wasn't resolved, somebody was going to jail.
He demanded that she gave an apology right then,
To make it known and bring it to an end.
A work relationship was how it began,
During lunch breaks she entertained my man.
An arrangement they hoped we'd never know,
When emotions got involved, she emitted a different glow.
Her lover confronted her, and it all came out,
The encounter brought on an unpleasant drought.
She was livid and questioned why he lied,
After the time they spent and the way she felt inside.
He said he wasn't sure if he wanted to leave,
Her reaction to what he said put a wrinkle in her sleeves.
She wanted the reassurance he had given her all along,
Her love for him erupted loudly in her tone.
He didn't appear to be emotionally attached,
Until she ran out crying and he ran behind her back,
I stood in disbelief, in a state of total shock,
And when he came back both doors were locked.

Mannequins

When I come across mannequins,
They don't say much,
They're quiet and cold,
Unresponsive to touch,
No heartbeats or thoughts,
Unable to clutch,
No movement in their feet,
Just fixed in awe,
Appearing to be flawless but stiffened with lockjaw.
The cynical intentions, meant only to disrupt,
A scrounger in disguise planning to corrupt.
Hoping to derail blessings and cause plans to fail,
Pretending in my face and still kissing my tail.
Like crabs in a bucket, pulling me down,
Hating to see me win and adjust my crown.

Demented love

The state of my cognition relies on you, you are my co-
dependent distraction,
My equilibrium settles in your presence.
Despite every alleged action my desires point in your
direction and I can't seem to remember why.
You are the hurricane in my brain, the reason for thoughts
untamed.
This is not normal and part of me knows, but I lack the
ability to process your conditional affection.
Catastrophic events often occur in my mind,
I'm not sure when it started, but it happens most of the
time.
Familiar actions guide thoughts of where, when, and who,
Triggered by assumptions and things you use to do.
Racing to place meaning deriving from an impaired
mindset between the margins.
Revisiting scenes that allude a production of pain
unintended to be pardoned.
Debris that blocks the cognitive ability to proceed.
Unwarranted accusations referenced from the past,
Sent by impulses from transmitters that alter the
hourglass,
Mental anguish depleted the nourishment needed to last.
Impervious to the need of aid and awareness of self,
Inscribing for fun and not to improve mental health.
Battling with and denying the realized truth,
Unconscious of the energy passed down to her youth.

The fear and anxiety of being judged,
A diagnosis of demented love.

Triggers

Most things around me serve as triggers,
My focus is wrong, and it figures.
I can never finish and that isn't good,
I need to do better, so I can get out of this hood.
Triggers come in different sizes and shapes,
They're unbiased, so they don't discriminate.
Activated by a depleted level of serotonin,
Managed by faith and the life that I'm owning,
I know what's good for me and what is not,
Triggers remove all the strength I've got.
I bob and weave when I see them near,
Trying to whisper past reminders in my ear,
I firmly refuse to give them the power,
I stand my ground because I'm not a coward.

Zaire

I felt your presence hovering over me at the top of the
staircase on thirty-third street.
The vibrations were different, and my heart was shattered,
but it did not let it show,
As I listened to dialogue from all the church folk;
Praising and praying, though I was tuned out,
As I sat in a daze, quiet as a mouse.

The house felt dark and enclosed like a cage,
Mourning was the expression taking center stage,
My family was affected, and I couldn't help,
Hoping to get ahold of a substance to relieve myself.
I pondered on the progression of his illness which led to
his death,
Thinking about all the ways I could have saved him myself.

Depression began to spread like a pandemic plague,
Staying to myself was the role that I craved,
A grave condition is what his body displayed.
His system shut down, and his energy dwindled.
I know something was wrong, the little smile I saw every
morning was gone.
I thought this would be simple.
A visit to the ER then moving right along.
In the bag was an outfit that was never worn.
With you music box you danced to, but there was no
rhythm in your feet.
The button was pressed, and you remained still,
That's when I realized this wasn't our normal drill,

It was hard to face, but I understood why,
They couldn't understand why my eyes remained dry,

One year later, I finally broke down,
Therapy was needed, but upon it, I frowned,
I held in the guilt, the hurt and the pain
I only had six months to call your name.

Zaire.

Still

It was too long for me to sit tight,
Strands of my hair started turning white,
So anxious to move, but I must stay still,
A struggle indeed because I have no chill,
What am I doing? I'm sick of it!
These games I'm playing, I need to quit,
It's my time to be selfish and process a change,
For me to take charge and dry up this rain,
To avoid the triggers and have control,
To put my goals in a serious stronghold.
To buckle down and execute my plan,
The only benefit to being still, is seeing where I stand.

Forty on One

I'm running on empty, I need to fill up,
Then I came to a stop, I was fresh out of luck,
What happen to my confidence?
Did you see where it went?
Emptiness filled the space inside,
I ran out of what I needed to drive.

It didn't matter what I had to do,
When I opened the trunk, I found a pair of boots.
I marched for a brief time heading uphill,
Just to find fuel to spin my wheels;
Not graded with an 87 or 93,
This fuel was custom-made for me.
At the top of the hill I found a store,
I sat down for a moment since my feet were sore.
I put forty on one and anxiously turned around,
Heading back to my destination, then he asked, "why the
frown".
I looked at him strangely and tilted my head,
Wondering about what he just said.
He went on to say, you have the overflow you deserve,
Let it pour inside of you, then go out and serve.
I smiled and quickly headed for the door,
Looking forward to my breakthrough, I rushed out of the
store.
As I got closer to my car, I felt the determination bubbling
inside,
When I poured the fuel in, I saw myself thrive,
I was sure it would go when I put it in drive.

I pulled off on a mission to spread the good word,
I wanted everyone to know the wonderful message that I
heard.

So, I drove the uphill, but when I arrived nothing was
around,
Only tumbleweeds sitting high on the natural ground.
I saw a sign that said gas station permanently closed
ahead,
I knew I wasn't dreaming, so I must have been led.
The next gas station wasn't for another 25miles
The man who asked about my frown turned my life
around.

God has all the fuel I need.

His Frustration

The cause was unclear,
Yet obvious to my intuition,
Lacking laughs, smiles, and much needed attention,
If I am your frustration, then who is not,
Your tone, so unfamiliar,
About me, you forgot,
Between us the air is not the same,
Sometimes I wonder if you remember my name,
Seasons have changed, and the leaves have turned,
Still, I release love, that hasn't been earned,
Not looking forward to a new day,
When actions of endearment have faded away,
Expressions of disgust along with vanished excitement,
Whatever his frustration is, I must be behind it,
The quick-tempered responses are where I find it,
Huffing and puffing, not listening at all,
Blame penetrating deep, resting in my flaws,
Underneath those clothes,
An abundance of lies,
Practiced reactions and bad vibes.

What's Best

We came from outside,
It was about to rain,
Our thoughts collided,
It was time for change,
I saw something in you that could not fuel my flame,
I chose to let go and lift the strain.
Rerouted to steer in the direction of happiness,
It took some time because I was a big mess.
The bruises weren't just wide, they ran deep,
An eye-opening moment provided much relief,
Loving myself is where it had to begin,
What's best for me may not be best for him.

High Discoveries

Before I shoot,
I never give it any thought,
No one around here cares to hear my thoughts,
Unless, I am talking that talk or walking that walk,
Us over here, we're unified in disguise,
Shelled upon friendliness,
With gloss in our eyes,
We light, we puff, and pop until our escape arrives,
Living a new day within the landmarks of the traffic maze,
Yearning for the ease of temporary joy,
Connected to unrealistic hopes used as a ploy,
Jittered energy calmed through inhalation,
Which prepares me for departure to the next destination,
Habitual behavior with no promising relief,
Most often cynical through the formation of high
discoveries.

My Candle

Before you told me, my nose was too wide,
Before the bruises I had to hide,
Before I was told what not wear,
Before I realized you didn't care,
Before I gained the strength to leave you back there.
Embodied confidence peaked once in a while,
Despite low self-esteem beneath the smile.
Still not strong enough to trust my own worth
I found solace in that place of hurt.
Forcing myself to remember good times we had,
Just to walk around and appear to be glad.
Reminiscing on what wasn't real from the start,
Overlooking the signs that should've dissuaded my heart.
The love I gave was more than you could handle,
But instead of loving me back you blew out my candle.

Toe to Toe

In a choke hold you go,
You better act like you know,
I'm not your foe, but I'm not your friend.
Don't get beside yourself,
I don't say things for my health.
From the womb you heard my voice,
So, respect is not a choice.
If I go toe to toe you'll get it in your chest,
I love you, but I don't play, so you better know what's
best.
Don't try me because I'll put you on the spot,
Don't you ever forget that I'm the only momma you got!

Different Gears

Do not be naive about his secrets,
He keeps them in his sleeve,
You want so much from him,
Beyond material things,
He understands your truth,
Though he constantly lies,
He told you what it was,
Still, on him you decide.
The moments you share are unplanned for a fleshly
connection,
He clears his scheduled and confirms you're the one he's
undressing;
You are his one and only during moments of release,
Still the temporary excitement never leaves you at peace;
Emotions unfold, and questions arise,
Then you ask yourself, what the future holds with this guy.
Forgetting about the power that you possess,
Quickly accommodating an intermittent caress.
Just enough to make you smile knowing there's an end to
this lifestyle.
When it's over, your eyes remain dry,
That's when you realize he'll never be the right guy.

Play It Safe

Cards down, cards down,
Don't move too fast,
If you tell him too much,
He'll repeat your past.

Wait a minute, wait a minute,
Girl you're doing too much;
Make him earn those treasures,
Don't just give them up.

You cook, and you clean, plus your credit is great,
Don't let him tamper with your heart you better play it
safe.

Conscientious

This isn't right,
I considered it twice,
Now, my mind and body are starting a fight,
Of course, my body is winning,
This flesh is so strong,
Most often, moving towards all the wrong,
Is it worth the devil's deal?
In my thoughts aren't where you belong,
Nor in my actions or even in this poem,
The middle is where I stand,
Between the halo and the thorn,
Then my conscientious asks, how's right different from
wrong.

Wind then the Rain

Trials will come, and you'll experience some pain,
Blowing you sideways making it hard to maintain;
Slowed by the wind, but growth from the rain
In an ever-changing world, elevating from the grain.
The current in constant circulation for change.
Be encourage by nature, the universe manifests your
gains.

Hydroplane

My life is spinning out of control,
When will it stop, I don't know,
I lost my ability I couldn't steer,
My body, shocked and shaking in fear.
Still I didn't shed a single tear.
Not a bruise or scratch after the hydroplane,
That's why I never neglect to call His name.

I will instruct you and teach you in the way you should go.
I will counsel you with my loving eye on you.
Psalms 32:8

Part 2: Tune up

Eye

Eye may get tired,
Eye may get distracted,
Eye may become frustrated and feel like giving up, but eye
know that my eyes are the windows to my soul. My
desires excrete through my pores. Even if the vision in one
eye is impaired, eye know that my goal is attainable
because eye made it believable, therefore it must be
achievable. Eye close my eyes each night and say a prayer
because eye continue to believe in what is not yet visible
to the naked eye.

Reactivated

The air I breath is different. I move through it without resistance. It all happened the day I woke up and began living my dream. Dreaming was not enough. Holding my desires captive, even if it meant dragging them through each level was no longer growth. I was awakened one morning by the sound of music coming from the complex next door. In that moment I found myself submerged in thoughts about the journey intended to circulate through my mind. I felt angry about the energy I continued to settle upon and anything in its path. I was frustrated with myself and desperate to find another approach. I was not where I imagined I would be, so my imagination began to fade, and my staircase followed. Procrastination kept me from maintaining peak performance in my areas of expertise. I had to reevaluate myself as well as my game plan. In doing so, I made a conscious effort to expand my mind and build my self-esteem by exercising positive thoughts and language. This helped me display confidence and gave me the confidence I needed to proceed into my purpose, my passion and to reach my highest potential. It reactivated my ambition.

Climb Out

Release the burdensome things that prevent the life you
want to live.
Start again and speak your truth,
Forgive what has caused distress,
Climb out of the mud,
Look forward and forget the rest.

You can do this,
You are amazing,
You are unstoppable,
You are creative,

Reintroduce yourself to yourself because you are the
person you vision yourself to be,
Just remember it starts down on bended knees.

Clinical Research

I am certain there were many before me.
And if genetics plays a part, then who am I saving?
My children, or maybe my grandchildren.
No more DSOMD screening,
On the higher power, I'm leaning.
I am hopeful and yes, I believe,
The chain will be broken, and mindsets will be freed.
Involvement and perseverance, a goal and a plan,
Clinical research and counseling to bring the generational
curse to an end.
Great achievements may not happen in a single day,
Just know that progress is merely a step away.
Understand that controlling your thoughts is not
something you win,
Having control is imperative to rebuking depression again.
It will creep up on you and try to come back,
You may forget it ever existed so when it comes, you'll be
thrown off track.
I don't want them to go through this, but I can't control
that.
I will give them an understanding and the name that they
should call,
HE will be there through the entire process and he them
through it all.
Don't be afraid, now you know what to do,
Eat healthy, exercise, join an activity and enroll in a class
or two,
Keep yourself going and don't take on issues that don't
belong to you.

Remember to lift your head high especially during a
difficult phase,
The person behind you is watching and taking notes for
better days.
I'm saving all my people.

My prayer is that none come after me.

Retaining Me

On a broken road, where the vison was cloudy.
Stuck with no strive and no desire to drive.
Unable to gain control or follow through,
Always unsure about what I should do.
Rock bottom is where I hit, but I was too far to quit.
My intent had to change, in chaos I remained.
Attempting to climb out of the cave, I had to be brave.
In a place of convenience, I stayed,
With internalizing thoughts, everything was my fault,
Retaining me in my journey to healing was the first step to
forgiving.

Expose Her

Tell them who she is,
Not who she pretends to be,
She walks the walk with a confident gab,
A waistline of responsibilities.
More than coils underneath those hats,
She organizes custom dreams;
To fulfill a plan, many won't understand
Lasting longer than material things

Today

Today I was encouraged by someone who looked like me.
I gave her a snippet of my story and she responded with
ample energy. Her words were refreshing, they activated
my drive.
She related to the challenges I held inside. I told her about
my book and her eyes grew wide.

Today I was encouraged by someone who looked like me.
We shared the same interest, but she released the strings.
We experienced the same obstacles; her perception was
her guide. She stopped living in fear, she no longer
wanted to hide.

Today I was encouraged by someone who looked like me.
She appeared out of nowhere with amazing energy. She
explained how she gained control and didn't look back.
She decided to keep going and stay on track.

Today I was encouraged by someone who looked like me.
She was capable because she was confident in her
abilities. She knew who to count on to keep her spirits
high. She knew God was faithful, even when she wanted
to cry. She was inspirational, and I wish she would've
stayed, but before she left, she said, catch up with me
some day.

She was me.☐

The Battle

This morning I sat in utter disbelief,
Communicating my thoughts directly to the Chief.
He said not to worry, the battle is not yours to fight,
I should've talked to him before I went to sleep last night.

Propel

Up, up to the sky
No limit when your committed, I'm ready to fly,
Tunnel vision has me spinning.
It's an amazing feeling, to have control,
The wait was long enough, so I'm retrieving my goal.
The message I'm sending, not fiction, only facts,
Starting with situations I dealt with way back,
The clock ticked loudly,
I had no time to waste,
I left a shoe behind,
Trying to run in the race.
Now things are looking up,
My life is aligned,
Given another chance by the divine.
A promising future gave me a sign, in bold letters it said,
it's my time.
Illuminating from a dark place and preparing to propel,
I'm claiming the next win,
That's right, I'm next to excel.

Degree of Love

Climb to the top of cloud nine.
While there, you'll see what it takes.
Love is not an overnight construction.
Through the levels you'll encounter mistakes.
Some will correlate and others you'll surpass,
Seeking fulfillment in Him, is a degree of love that will
always last.

Dear Fear,

When you are not around, she writes,
She escapes into the ambiance of the night.
Internal harmony sets the mood,
Enduring the past with great fortitude.

Submerged in her oohs,
Taken away by awes,
Despite her flaws this is no mirage.
Valiant in her truths,
Tirelessly writing during the arrival of the moon.

Sincerely,

Shandle

Band Aid

Confined to your abusive ways,
Stressed out and unable to sleep for days.
Accustomed to the situation,
I kept a box of band aids.
To cover all my hurt or give it some relief.
Patch up emotions to give

Make Y'all Proud

Ever since I was a child,
There was never a need for a crowd,
Mommy and daddy were the ones allowed.
The reasons I know that I will be ok,
The reasons I try not to worry and pray.
The reasons why I proceeded,
The fear faced a stampede.
Proving that I'm capable always stuck with me,
I wanted you to see that I could stand on my own two feet.
All I ever wanted to do was make y'all proud of me.

Next Level

I'm high and I know this,
I'm high as a kite,
Ready to smoke another one,
Before the end of the night.
My boyfriend is getting on my nerves, but I let him slide,
That's how I know, I got to be high.
Now, let me change the subject,
I want to keep it real,
I'm ready for an excursion, and I need a good deal.
My smile grows wide and tears form slow,
Because they deserve more than what they currently
know,
Enclosed emotions they'll never see,
Sealed and only made visible to me.
Aiming to show them the next level of this thing called life,
They deserve it all, so I must get it right.

Chain Reaction

My reaction to life events that kept me bound by a chain.

Seclusion...

Dividing me from life through dejection and tarnishing my name,
Isolating myself was my reaction to the challenge of unexpected life events,
Though, I was never alone because He is always in my presence,
Guiding and strengthening me along the way,
The company I need to start my day.

For I know the plans I have for you declares the Lord; plans to prosper you and not to harm you, plans to give you hope and a future

Jeremiah 29:11

Part 3: Living Unapologetically

God, only you can supply my array of needs. Thank you for direction, clarity, and understanding.

Baby Oil

This morning I was served breakfast in bed by a chocolate brother with jet black hair. He came into the room wearing gray sweatpants and no shirt. He gently touched my shoulder and said, "honey it's time to get up". As I opened my eyes, he stared me in the eyes and smiled. He said, "good morning" and kissed me on the forehead. When I began to speak, he placed his index finger over my lips to silence me. He grabbed a piece of fruit and fed it to me. His body was glistening as if he'd put on an entire bottle of baby oil. He continued feeding me breakfast while sitting on the edge of the bed looking like a model sent from heaven. When I finished, he quickly stood up to take my plate into the kitchen. On the way into the kitchen he fell. I quickly ran to him, wondering if he was ok. It appeared that he slipped and hit his head. I tried to wake him, but there was no response. I called 911 and said, "please hurry he's unresponsive". Seven minutes later the paramedics arrived, but it was too late. He was already gone. I screamed, no! Why? My chocolate! Since then I have not been the same. Relationships have been extremely hard for me.

The cause of death was too much baby oil on the body. Specifically, on his feet. Had he put on socks this would have never happened. I always wondered how his skin was so much softer than mine. I checked the bottle and it was half empty.

Transaction History

If I end up in the back ward they won't care,
They won't visit me, they'll walk by and stare;
They'll say, remember her,
Then point and laugh,
I'll follow my shadow and hide behind my past.

I can't go backwards,
I'll have no way out,
There's no love in that air,
Just lies and doubt,
Tricks minus the treats,
Negative vibes from people I wish I didn't meet,
Stuck in a zone where I didn't belong,
It was always bittersweet.
Right never made it and I left with no regrets,
Listening more than I speak,
Creating a new season to invest in my happiness.

Reveal

I pulled the sheet,
It had me covered down to my feet;
It was thick and warm,
The gauze that protected me when I was torn;
Often misunderstood, but my intentions are always good,

Forced to reveal this woman of steel,
In a state that made me far less ill.
With my head held high registering astute observations,
I ready to make use of my education.

Grocery List

I was bored one day,
I had nothing to do,
During times like this I mostly think about food.
It's the Taurus in me made an educated guess,
When food is on my mind I forget about the rest.
I made a list of things that I wanted to create,
I wanted to put a snack on my porcelain plate.
My grocery list was extensive, but not that expensive;
No influences around, so I drifted into snack town.
Caught up in thoughts surrounded by food, so I wondered
a lot.

I felt more stable, when I brought food to the table.

PMS

I am in the writing mood tonight.
Nothing special on my mind,
I'm not even trying to rhyme,
But I strive to deliver every time.
The best of the best, that poetry bump and grind;
If you don't understand, you may have to read it twice,
I'm totally amazing, completely out of sight,
My poetic mental state keeps me awake all night.

Plan B

To see you again after so long,
Brought back memories of times we shared alone.
Surprised to see you in this much pain,
After choosing to change another's name.
I'm too amazing to be your plan B,
So, this serves as closure for me.

Key

I have the key,
It was given;
To open the doors appointed specifically for me.

Declined

I don't want my past back,
I see it looking from afar,
Lurking in the darkness,
Sitting in that tinted car;
I don't want my past back,
My past can't rescue me;
It separates me from greatness,
Dissociating my identity.
Declined is what I tell it, as it tries to draw me in,
Reminding me of my faults and revisiting my sins.
I appreciate my past, it has taught me well,
My future is greater; therefore, I cannot fail,
The battle was never mine, I was made to prevail.
What kept me from believing?
Smothered in goals I was not achieving.
I don't want my past back, I will not revert.

Reign

In a world infused with test,
The company of you is always best,
I come and go, but you stay the same,
Enduring to complete my mission and umbrella your reign.

Natural Ability

The ocean is flowing,
Grass is growing,
Babies being born,
Constant motion,
The fullness of the moon shines so bright,
Leading us into a restful night.
The whisper of the wind gliding pass,
Gently kissing the tips of the grass.
As if there was a secret to tell.

Fixated

Walking through the tunnel with 20/20 vision,
My eyes are on the prize because I made my decision,
To improve every day, even when it gets tough,
There are times when I feel that I don't do it enough.
Pressuring myself to improve as I turn the page,
Respecting the process and learning in every stage.
The draft that is constant and helps me pick up speed,
It is something I want and most definitely a need.
Directed to this place of focus through ample evidence,
Fixated on my passion because it makes so much sense.

Five-Star Attitude

No, I won't settle,
I want an upgrade,
Last year in this position, is where I stayed.
Things have changed, and I don't mean to be rude,
But you're talking to a woman with a five-star attitude.

I want more, and it will happen for me.
The desires of my heart are too large for you to see.

23 Books

37 minus 14 is 23,
14 was the age I discovered poetry,
The saying is, good things come to those who wait,
23 years ago, I dealt with my first heartbreak,
After 37 years things have turned around,
I could have written 23 books, between then and now,
But my 14-year-old mind was not that advanced,
Those 23 attempts didn't stand a chance,
I refuse to live in 23 years of regret,
That 14-year-old hadn't gone through much yet,
As I look back from a 37-year young point of view,
There is something about the number 23 that generates
my mood,
Out of all the many hours in the day,
23 stands out, it paves my way,
Completing 23 books is the intended goal,
Writing is intriguing, it fills my soul.

My Best

It's what I was raised to do.
If I don't try, I'll never know what it'll lead me to;
I'll never know what could be, if I don't give it my best,
Life is too short to throw my hands up and fail another
test.

Greatness

It is no secret,
The blueprint that guides us through life,
Directing the path as we orbit this world.
Hurry not,
Mimic the moon,
Allow greatness to come,
Don't give up too soon.
What is meant will always be,
There are possibilities for what you do not see.

Mother

My mother supplies comfort when I'm feeling down,
She's the one who's there when nobody is around;
Her unconditional love is shown each day,
She's who I talk to when I'm not sure about what to say;
She's that special person that I always keep close,
Every turn I make, she's at her post;
She knows when I'm hurt, and she shows concern,
She taught me several lessons that I've already learned;
Passing along wisdom because she already knows,
Instilling confidence and keeping me on my toes.
Sometimes she'll say things that I don't want to hear,
It's her way of navigating tough love into my ears.

Take care of your mother, she covers you in prayer,
When everyone leaves, she'll still be right there.

Connected

Loving without boundaries whether the sun shines or not,
Understanding and protecting the bond that you've got,
Projecting compassion and communicating concerns,
Listening attentively because it's the only way you'll learn.
Contributing to the growth of the circle you formed,
Covering each other throughout each storm;
Supplying guidance with zeal and zest,
Living in the moment and cherishing the rest.

Daddy

My safety lives in you.
The fairytale dreams,
You made them all come true.
Your lectures make me cry, but never for long,
I drank all my milk just to show you that I am strong.
The realities of the world,
You tried to keep them hidden,
Then one day you realized I could make big girl decisions.
Your concern is hard to hide,
It shows in your voice,
At least until I assure you that I made the right choice.
You don't have to worry,
Because I am ok,
Nothing is holding me back or standing in my way.

YOU

Love you,
Be you,
Know you,
Uplift you,
Do it for you,
Celebrate you,
Spend time with you,
Take care of you,
Put you first,
Pamper you,
Express you,
Respect you,
Trust you,
Never doubt you,
Believe in you,
Never give up on you,
Be true to you,
Listen to you,
Understand you,
Know what's best for you,
Make you happy,
Give you all that you've got because you never know
where it'll take you.

3 Words

Healthy
Healthy living is a lifestyle.

Purposeful
Purposeful living is necessary.

Knowledgeable
Gain knowledge each day you live. Education should be ongoing.

Laugh

Laughter extends your years,
It wipes away those tears.
It pulls you from under those sheets,
It keeps you hopeful and upbeat,
An expression indeed even in disbelief,
Laugh more each day as the hands turn,
Always be mindful of the lessons you learn.
Laugh more.

Finish

Finish that diploma,
Finish that degree,
Finish eating that plate of peas,
Finish what you've started and never give up,
Finish, even when you think that you're stuck.

Finish that project,
Don't throw it to the side.
Years from now, you'll find it in the files you hide.

Hey you, just finish,
Don't be afraid,
Finish your mission and everything will be ok.

It's ok

It's ok to leave your past behind,
Keep on pushing,
You'll be just fine.

Turning Adversities Around

Challenges are upon us during every season of our lives. They coexist in nature, but we should never allow them to keep us inanimate. We were made in an image of greatness; therefore, we should not be controlled by thoughts or people that make us feel incapable.

There are many mental health challenges, examples include problems with anxiety, depression, attention deficit hyperactivity disorder (ADHA), autism, post-traumatic stress disorder (PTSD), schizophrenia, and bi-polar disorder. These disorders affect people differently, causing them to feel anxious, nervous, and overwhelmed by feelings of sadness or making it hard to them to focus. These disorders change how you think, feel and behave.

It is important to be accurately diagnosed by a mental health professional. Several bad days does not equate to a mental health disorder. If you believe you have a mental health illness, it is important to talk to someone you trust. This is the first step to getting better and changing your mindset.

Acknowledgements

I am internally grateful. Thank you, Ron Graphics, for capturing the essence of me through photography and graphic design. To my artistic brother Crigh Edward Chapman thank you for supplying innovative artwork through your unique point of view. To my brother Antonio F. Moody thank you for taking time to collaborate and provide a well written mental health reflection. To my Mother Ann Chapman, thank you for the inspirational theological reflection and for your assistance with formatting. To DSuave thank you for your timeliness, patience and for capturing an amazing professional photo.
I am grateful for all your contributions.

Photography/Graphic Design: Ron Images
IG: ron_images

Creative Artwork: Crigh Edward Chapman
Cri Chapman Art
crichapmanart.com
IG: artcrudddcri

Mental Health reflection: Antonio F. Moody
Licensed Graduate
Professional Counselor

Theological reflection & formatting:
Ann Chapman
B.A. in Biblical Studies

Photography: D. Suave
Dsuave.com

eBook edition available through Kindle

Subscribe to Shandles' website and social media pages to be one of the first to receive information about new book releases and book signings.

ShandleWrites.com
Facebook: Shandle Writes
Instagram: Shandle_writes

Made in the USA
Lexington, KY
10 November 2019